Original title:
A Basket of Fruitful Days

Copyright © 2025 Creative Arts Management OÜ
All rights reserved.

Author: Adeline Fairfax
ISBN HARDBACK: 978-1-80586-372-4
ISBN PAPERBACK: 978-1-80586-844-6

Echoes of Blossoms and Bearers

The sun does dance, and so do we,
With fruit in hand and glee, you see!
A pear in pockets, a peach on heads,
We trot along, our laughter spreads.

Bananas slip as we all trip,
An orange roll, oh what a flip!
Coconuts bounce like merry souls,
In a game of fruit, we reach our goals.

Serendipity Under the Canopy

Under the trees, we skip and sway,
Mango dreams light up our play.
A cherry pie just flew away,
We'll catch our treats before end of day!

Lemons giggle from their perch,
While berries huddle, plotting a search.
A kiwi whispers, 'Join the fun!'
As we chase them under the sun.

The Colorful Tapestry of Hours

A tapestry we weave with cheer,
Grapes do tumble, let's give a cheer!
With wacky hats made of ripe fruit,
We'll parade around in silly pursuit.

Peaches laughing, nectarines sing,
As we dance through this vibrant fling.
Apple jokes and citrus puns,
Spin us around till the day is done.

Petals in the Afternoon Light

Petals flutter, soft and bright,
A watermelon slice? What a sight!
We juggle seeds with goofy grins,
As laughter thickens, the fun begins.

Strawberry crowns upon our heads,
We march like kings, as laughter spreads.
In the afternoon's warm embrace,
We find our joy in this silly race.

Citrus Echoes of Happiness

Lemons laugh from morning light,
Oranges dance and feel just right.
Grapefruits giggle, share a wink,
Bananas slip and start to think.

Juicy jokes in every slice,
Peels and puns both feel so nice.
Limes throw shade with cheeky glee,
Fruits unite, a comedy.

Harvest of Sunlit Moments

Berry tales sung by the breeze,
Peachy puns that aim to please.
Melons roll with mirth and mirage,
Kiwis plot a fruity collage.

Tomatoes share a salsa spree,
Corny lines are totally free.
Sunny days in laughter's hold,
Grapes weave stories bright and bold.

The Orchard of Yesterdays

Apple memories on display,
Cherries giggle, hip hooray!
Nostalgia swings from limb to limb,
Past the cider, tales begin.

Rusty swings and laughter's chime,
Fruits recall their prime-time rhyme.
Joyful bugs at dusk parade,
Buzzing light, a sweet charade.

Whispers of the Ripened Grove

Under trees, the jokes are ripe,
Peelings shared in every type.
Freshly plucked and lightly tossed,
Punchlines grow, none are lost.

Squirrels chuckle up above,
Fruits abound, a light-hearted shove.
Nature's punchline, sweet delight,
In the grove, we laugh all night.

Mirrored Reflections of Joy

In the morning sun I found,
A woeful grape that rolled around.
It laughed at me with little flair,
Fell into jam, no longer bare.

The oranges wore a silly grin,
As lemons danced with zestful spin.
Together they made quite a scene,
Juicy jokes that burst so clean.

Layers of Lush Experiences

Beneath the leaf, a berry peeked,
With secrets sweet, it softly squeaked.
The cantaloupe said, 'Join the fun!'
'I'm no mere melon, I'm the pun!'

A pineapple wore a crown so tall,
But slipped on juice, had quite a fall.
Outrageous laughter filled the stand,
As fruity chaos ruled the land.

Harvesting Hope from Ancient Trees

The apple tree stood proud and wise,
With tales of cider in disguise.
It whispered leaves of funny lore,
And gifted pies we all adore.

The old oak chuckled with the breeze,
'I've seen it all, just take your tease!'
Through nuts and seeds of jolly cheer,
I learned that laughter's always near.

Flavors of Existence Intertwined

Banana peels laid out in style,
Challenging walkers to a smile.
With every slip, there's fun to bake,
In this vibrant fruity wake.

The mixed bowl danced in colors bright,
With every bite, a wacky sight.
Peachy giggles echoed high,
As fruity flavors soared the sky.

Colorful Gatherings of Existence

In the garden, giggles grow,
Bananas wear hats, don't you know?
Apples juggle smiles with flair,
While grapes roll on, without a care.

Peaches play tag, what a sight,
Oranges bounce, oh, what a flight!
Lemons laugh in sunny light,
Making each moment feel just right.

Chronicles of a Sun-Drenched Day

Under the sun, berries dance,
Every melon takes its chance.
Cherries throw a party loud,
While pineapples feel oh so proud.

Kiwis wave from rustic trees,
With nature's laughter in the breeze.
Watermelons roll, giggle, and spin,
A fiesta of flavor, let the fun begin!

Radiant Blessings from Nature's Table

A cantaloupe cracks a cheeky grin,
As figs join in, their sweet violin.
Each berry whispers silly tales,
While nuts cheer loudly with their gales.

Pears hopping in a feathered dance,
Ripe avocados join in their chance.
With every crunch, a chuckle springs,
Celebrating life and all its flings.

Vineyards of Lived Experience

Gathered grapes in a merry bunch,
Crack jokes at the vine's big lunch.
A vintage laugh, they toast with glee,
While plump figs sway like it's all free.

As the vines weave tales of delight,
Of sunlit hours and laughter bright.
With every sip of life's sweet wine,
We toast to moments so divine.

Slices of Eternity

In a world where bananas dance,
Apples wear a glitzy pants.
Oranges juggle, quite absurd,
Lemon laughs, it's absolutely stirred.

Berries gossip, what a scene,
Pineapple's crown, a noble green.
Together they frolic without cares,
Chasing dreams in fruity airs.

Breath of Fruity Horizons

Kiwi's singing tunes divine,
Grapes form trios, oh, how they shine!
Tasting joy on every tongue,
Mango winks, our hearts are young.

Peachy giggles roll like waves,
Raspberry rebels, oh, how they rave!
Watermelon splashes all around,
In this fruity, fun-filled ground.

Medleys of Flavorful Wanderings

Cherries chase the morning light,
Figs play hopscotch, what a sight!
Plums tell tales of summer's cheer,
Each story sweeter with every beer.

Coconut, the beach bum king,
Dances on the sand, let's all sing!
With fruity friends, we roam so free,
Life's a smoothie, just wait and see.

Vibrance in Every Turn

Grapefruit laughs, it's quite the tease,
Dates throw parties with such ease.
Citrus dreams and stylish flair,
Pomegranate pearls float in the air.

Lime's twisty jokes make us groan,
Guess who's coming, Apple's grown!
In this harvest we all connect,
With funny vibes, what's next, we'll expect!

Nurtured Through Time's Embrace

In the garden where laughs collide,
A tomato slipped, oh, what a ride!
The onions giggle, quite a sight,
While carrots dance in morning light.

With every seed, a joke was sown,
A cucumber spins, feeling quite grown.
The squash rolls by with a wink and a grin,
As bees crack puns while buzzing in.

The Essence of Sun-Drenched Paths

Bananas peel with such great flair,
While pears complain, it's simply not fair.
Oranges chuckle, a citrus choir,
Singing tunes that never tire.

The sunbeams play, a tag, a tease,
Melons giggle in the breeze.
Each stroll brings laughter, bright and loud,
Fruitful days, we're all quite proud!

A Symphony of Harvested Hues

A peach cries out, "I'm too ripe, oh dear!"
While cherries blush, bursting with cheer.
Grapes gossip low, swinging on vines,
Eager for stories at sunset's signs.

The figs drop puns, sticky and sweet,
As berries bump in a fruity beat.
Nature's laughter echoes through,
In a joyous mix of every hue.

Dreams Plucked from Morning Dew

With dew on leaves, the magic's bright,
Strawberries giggle in the soft twilight.
Lemons chuckle, sour but wise,
As smoothies whirl under the skies.

Each dawn brings a fresh and funny tale,
Of apples tripping down the trail.
Let's toast to mornings full of play,
In this lush land, we laugh away.

Memories Folded in Petals

In gardens bright, we rolled on grass,
Chasing dreams as hours passed.
With lemonade spills on sunny days,
We danced and laughed in silly ways.

A kite flew high, then took a dive,
We raced the wind, felt so alive.
In hats too big, we made our stand,
A parade of giggles, hand in hand.

The Aroma of Lush Adventures

Sniffing out mischief, we took the chance,
In a treehouse high, we'd plot and prance.
With cookies stolen, sweet surprise,
We cracked up loud, laughter in our eyes.

The mud pies served with pride and flair,
With dirt-streaked faces, we didn't care.
A treasure hunt for candy gold,
Each bite a story, sweetly told.

Threads of Golden Light

Casting shadows in evening glow,
We wove our tales, the stars below.
With silly songs and bursts of cheer,
We made the night our own frontier.

In twilight's grip, we raced the night,
With fireflies casting sparks of light.
Organs of laughter—who could keep still?
Each moment woven with pure thrill.

Growing Echoes of Laughter

Sprouting dreams in fields of fun,
We shouted joy till day was done.
With silly hats and painted toes,
The laughter bubbled; joy just grows.

We played in puddles, splashed our way,
Never knowing it was just play.
Echoes of giggles, light as air,
In every heartbeat, memories share.

Memories Plucked from Vines

In the garden of time, we laughed and played,
Grapes of joy hanging, never delayed.
With each pluck and munch, a giggle arose,
'Twas a fruit-fueled party, as everyone knows.

Cherries danced with cheeks so round,
Mischief sipped nectar, not quite profound.
Every bite a chuckle, every sip a grin,
In this vine-ripened world, let laughter begin.

Sweets of Existence on Serene Paths

Honey drips slow from the morning trees,
While squirrels plot nibbles with cheeky ease.
Cookies of sunshine, baked to delight,
Even the sunlight seems to giggle outright.

Lemonade rivers twist and swirl,
Splashing sweet joy in a sugary whirl.
With every sip, the world turns bright,
Sweets of existence make everything right.

Paths Paved with Colorful Illumination

Bright marigolds giggle as they sway in the breeze,
Tickled by daisies and picnic ants tease.
Every color a joke, every hue a song,
With paths paved in laughter, you simply can't go wrong.

The sun wore sunglasses, oh what a sight,
Bananas in shorts as they danced in delight.
Rainbows paraded, each color a jest,
In this vibrant town, humor is the best.

Blessings Within the Orchard of Life

Apple trees whisper tales full of cheer,
Pears with punchlines make laughter appear.
A dance of peaches, a jig of the figs,
Silly old orchard, full of life's digs.

Cider flows freely like thoughts in a jam,
Every day's bounty is grandma's grand slam.
Ripening moments, all sunny and goofy,
With blessings so sweet, life's juicy and woofy.

Savoring the Sweetness of Now

Oh, I tripped on a banana peel,
My laughter echoed, quite surreal.
With apples talking, pears in tune,
They danced around a watermelon moon.

Juggling oranges, what a sight!
Pineapple hats, we feel so bright.
The grapes are gossiping, oh what fun,
Chasing after the setting sun.

Melons giving life advice,
"Don't take it too seriously, be nice!"
Strawberries giggling, in a sweet row,
With every joke, the juices flow.

So here we are, in carefree play,
Eating our moments, come what may.
Each silly slip is just a part,
Of how we savor life, oh heart!

Radiant Moments in the Light

A lemon squirt, oh what a tease,
Sunshine bursts and hearty wheeze.
Peaches blush with stories to share,
While cherries giggle beyond compare.

The citrus clouds float in the air,
Poking fun without a care.
Limes pull faces, cheeky and bright,
While apricots bask in the light.

With pomelo puns as our muse,
We laugh till our sides start to bruise.
Bananas jiggle, 'what's this all about?'
Fruitful zeal, we laugh and shout!

So when you feel life might be a drag,
Join the fruit crew, grab your swag.
For in each morsel, a treasure we find,
Radiant moments, one of a kind!

The Palette of Lived Days

In a bowl of colors, joy we mix,
The laughter ripples, just for kicks.
Pine cones chuckle, apples stack high,
Throw in a mango, watch spirits fly!

Grapefruits giggle with zest and flair,
"Do pears pick their outfits with care?"
Caught in a tangle of twinkling vines,
Where cherries make the best punch lines.

Life's canvas splashed with silly spree,
Each hue a memory, wild and free.
Kiwi quips beneath the sun's glow,
We create our art, take it slow.

So let's paint our joy, day by day,
With fruit and laughter leading the way.
A splash of humor, colors so bright,
In the palette of days, pure delight!

Branches of Joyful Reflection

Under the tree of jolly thought,
Lemons grinning with wisdom sought.
Kiwis flutter, with giggles they sway,
Sharing stories of a witty play.

Branches heavy with laughter's load,
Fruits spinning tales as they explode.
"Who knew life could be such a treat?"
With ripe banter, we dance to the beat.

Mangoes whisper sweet, 'Life's a game,'
"If you slip, just laugh, it's all the same!"
Pears toss puns from heights so grand,
Joyful reflections, hand in hand.

So let us gather beneath this shade,
With fruit and folly, be unafraid.
For in every moment, a story unfolds,
On branches of laughter, life beholds!

Petals of Time in Full Bloom

In the garden of giggles, we sway,
Each petal a memory, bright and gay.
Laughter sprinkles like morning dew,
Tickling our souls, just me and you.

With sneakers on, we dance through the grass,
Catching the moments, let time pass.
Like bouncing berries, we tumble around,
In this playful world, true joy is found.

Through the years, our hair turns gray,
Yet, silliness lingers, come what may.
We'll chase the clouds, eat ice cream with glee,
In our patch of sunlight, forever free.

So here's to the blooms, bright and absurd,
In the silly symphony, our hearts are stirred.
With petals of time, let's twirl and tease,
For it's the moments that truly please.

The Abundance of Shared Moments

Two peas in a pod, that's how we roll,
Chasing the sunsets, making us whole.
A picnic of laughter, sandwiches too,
With funny tales of the past we brew.

Where lemonade rivers twist and flow,
And every mishap is a comedic show.
We trip over roots, but laugh 'til we cry,
In the orchard of life, we reach for the sky.

Banana peels slip in our path,
But we dance in circles, and provoke a laugh.
With every silly face and playful pun,
The tapestry of joy has just begun.

So raise your glass to friendship's tune,
Under the watchful gaze of the moon.
For in this abundance, we find our place,
In the banquet of moments, we share with grace.

Seasons of Delicious Reveries

In spring, we blossom, a vibrant spree,
With petals flapping like fish in the sea.
Sunshine's a cookie, warm and bright,
We nibble on dreams, sharing daylight.

Summer's a melon, sweet and sublime,
With splashes of laughter, we dance in time.
Watermelon seeds fly, and giggles ignite,
As we play tag with shadows, delight in flight.

Autumn leaves tumble, in crunch we trust,
Collecting gold coins, in laughter we rust.
With pumpkin spice lattes, we huddle and chat,
Sharing goofy tales, while donning a hat.

Winter is cocoa, extra marshmallows, please,
With snowball fights and tickle-induced wheezes.
In each season's embrace, we twirl and sway,
Creating a harvest of joyous play.

Fruits of Life's Potent Elixirs

Life's a smoothie, whipped and whirled,
Ingredients crazy, that twist and twirled.
Bananas and berries, in laughter we blend,
A concoction of joy, around every bend.

We squeeze out the citrus, zest so bright,
Infusing our days with giggles and light.
Like cherries on top, the silliness grows,
In this fizzy mix, our happiness flows.

Every hiccup a gift, each stumble a score,
As we sprinkle our days with humor galore.
With grapes of mischief, we toast to the ride,
In this wild fruit punch, laughter's our guide.

So let us sip slowly, savor the fun,
With each fruity moment, our hearts become one.
For life's potent blend is a jolly parade,
In the flavors of friendship, we'll never fade.

Reaping the Gentle Fragrance

In the garden, I found a peach,
It looked so ripe, just within reach.
I thought to munch, what a delight,
But it rolled away, what a sight!

Oh, bananas dancing in the breeze,
They wave at me, oh, such a tease.
I tried to catch them, what a blunder,
One slipped away, then there was thunder!

Grapes in clusters, laughing with glee,
They tickled my nose, oh woe is me!
I tried to pick, but they fought back,
With each pluck, I fell off track!

Around the trees, the apples grin,
They play hide and seek, it's a win!
I took a swing, felt like a champ,
But missed my mark; I'm now a stamp!

Embrace of Nature's Kaleidoscope

In the orchard, vibes prevail,
Berries laughing, tell a tale.
One berry said, "I've got your back,"
While another rolled, causing a crack!

Oranges in a frisky sprint,
I giggled hard, oh what a hint.
Zesty puns they threw around,
And soon my laughter did abound!

The pears wore hats, quite absurd,
Said, "Life is a fruit—just look at the bird!"
I pondered hard, cracked a smile,
Can fruits crack jokes? Just for a while!

The cherries twirled in a merry dance,
Invited me, gave fate a chance.
I joined the fun, but fell on my face,
Now I'm the fruit of a silly race!

Tapestry of Colorful Tomorrows

A rainbow fruit sat high on a shelf,
I thought it spoke, was that myself?
It winked at me with a juicy smile,
And said, "Come join, stay for a while!"

Each lemon laughed, oh such a scene,
Such sour faces, but they were keen.
They squeezed out jokes, zest in the air,
I almost choked, joy's a rare fare!

The kiwis juggled, quite the show,
I can't compete, my talent's low.
They tossed and turned, bursting with cheer,
While I just tripped, forgot my fear!

The fruit parade rolled into view,
A marching band in colors so true.
But I had to leave, my time was done,
Fare thee well, this fruity fun!

Canvas of Juicy Memories

Remember when we reached the top,
To grab those fruits—we couldn't stop?
A watermelon slipped, oh joy, oh dread,
It bounced right off, now it's surely wed!

The lychee laughed as I took a bite,
Its squishy softness brought pure delight.
But it squirted juice, right up my nose,
I laughed so hard, how the laughter rose!

The plums played tag—oh what a chase,
I tripped and tumbled, fell on my face.
Yet their sweet giggles filled the air,
Making my fall a comical flare!

At day's end, we basked in the glow,
Of fruity chaos and a light-hearted flow.
Memory's bright, like colors of candy,
Even the failings turned out quite dandy!

Harvesting Heartfelt Moments

In the orchard, laughter roams,
We gather smiles like wayward gnomes.
Sunshine drips from every tree,
It's a burst of bliss, just wait and see.

Juicy jokes hang from each branch,
Who knew that life could give such a chance?
Giggles mix with the soft rustle,
As we munch on fruit and flex our muscle.

Shadows dance like silly sprites,
Chasing dreams on summer nights.
With every bite, a chuckle shared,
Moments sweet, nothing compared.

Harvesting joy, we swing and sway,
Gathering greens on a sunlit day.
In this garden, we play our part,
Savoring laughter, filling the heart.

Lush Layers of Existence

Beneath the layers, laughter hides,
In every fruit, a giggle resides.
Peeling away the silly skins,
To find the joy that always wins.

Bananas slip, oranges bounce,
Who knew fruit could make us flounce?
A watermelon, big and round,
Grows a grin with every sound.

A bunch of grapes begins to sway,
As funny faces come out to play.
Layered laughs, a tasty treat,
Layers of fun beneath our feet.

In this tapestry of delight,
Every nibble sparks the light.
Fruitful days, a comic chase,
With every slice, we find our place.

Breezes of Rustic Delight

Rustic winds whisper tales so bright,
Of pie-eating contests under starlight.
Fruits rolling by, oh what a sight,
In this orchard, joy takes flight.

Breezes tickle, apples fall,
Who made that noise? Was it a call?
Cherries giggle, peaches spin,
Nature's chuckles, let the fun begin!

Laughter flows like rivers wide,
Sliding down the hill with pride.
Barefoot frolic, splashes loud,
In our patch of fun, we're proud.

As we gather, let's make a cheer,
For every fruit and friend held dear.
In breezy spins and funny flights,
We harvest joy in playful sights.

Glistening Pearls of Time

Elderly trees, wise as can be,
Dropping jewels for you and me.
Each shiny fruit a story told,
Glistening pearls, a sight to behold.

With every pick, a tale unspools,
As laughter tumbles, breaking rules.
Oranges dance in a zesty rush,
In the golden hour, we'll never hush.

Time's sweet nectar drips from vines,
Wrinkled hands, but oh, what finds!
Fruitful days steeped in glee,
Moments cherished—come laugh with me!

Glistening memories, bright and warm,
Like ripened fruits before a storm.
Together we reap, side by side,
In this orchard, where dreams abide.

Chasing Shadows of Golden Hours

The sun's a lazy cat, it rolls,
Chasing light as laughter strolls.
Each hour a new game that we play,
With shadows dancing, come what may.

Fleeting moments, caught and tossed,
Like candy wrappers, they're not lost.
We gather giggles, snorts, and sighs,
In this circus of time 'neath sunny skies.

Tick-tock tickles, what a tease,
Time's a wind that wiggles with ease.
We run around, it never waits,
Still, we stumble through our fates.

With every wink the day does pass,
A raucous fun, as we amass.
So here we'll dance without a care,
In golden hours, laughter fills the air.

Fruits of Time's Tender Embrace

Life's a fruit stand with colors bright,
Bananas laughing, apples light.
Pineapples wear a crown quite proud,
A giggling bunch, unruly crowd.

Grapes are whispers, rolling in lines,
Cherries wink, tasting like wines.
Peaches giggle, tickled and sweet,
While lemons pucker, can't take the heat.

Each bite a chuckle, each laugh a cheer,
In this orchard of joy, crystal clear.
We pluck and grin, make juice from our play,
In the sweetest embrace of each funny day.

So let's feast on smiles, fresh from the vine,
In this zany garden where our hearts entwine.
With laughter as our morning's cheer,
We celebrate time, year after year.

Sweet Juices of Memory's Bounty

A jar of giggles grins from the shelf,
Each one a memory, shared with oneself.
Sipping sweetness, trust the past,
In laughter's glow, forever cast.

Sticky fingers and smiles abound,
Each memory's juice, a joy profound.
Peels of laughter wrapped up tight,
In every sip, a spark of light.

Harness the fun like a playful breeze,
Dancing through days, with perfect ease.
Each drop an adventure, bold and new,
With flavors of silly, just for you.

So raise a glass to joy, so bold,
In a tapestry of tales to be told.
A banquet of smiles, let's reel it in,
With sweet, juicy memories, let the fun begin!

Lullabies of Flourishing Seasons

Oh, the seasons hum their gentle tune,
Whispers of spring, bright like a balloon.
Summer winks with a cheeky grin,
While fall throws leaves in a playful spin.

Winter giggles beneath blankets white,
Snowflakes dance in the soft moonlight.
Each season sings, some highs, some lows,
In this rascally show where laughter grows.

Buds are bursting, and blooms appear,
Nature's laughter fills the atmosphere.
As we sway to the rhythm of days,
In this merry waltz of delightful ways.

So hold on tight, let the music play,
With joy in our hearts, come what may.
In the tapestry of time's embrace,
We'll dance through seasons, finding our place.

Chronicles from the Heart's Orchard

In the orchard where laughter grows,
Apples giggle with rosy toes.
Bananas slip on sunny beams,
While oranges burst with silly dreams.

Pears hold secrets, ripe with fun,
Plotting tricks beneath the sun.
Cherries dance upon the breeze,
Making merry with silly keys.

Grapes wear glasses, acting wise,
Underneath the bluest skies.
Lemons squeeze out sunshine bright,
Joking as they roll in flight.

Peaches, plump with jokes to share,
Throwing puns into the air.
In this grove of giddy play,
Every fruit knows how to sway.

Glimmers of Light through the Canopy

Beneath the branches, shadows dance,
Fruits reveal their hidden chance.
Mangoes winking with a grin,
Whispering secrets sweet within.

Lemons laugh at passing bees,
While figs tickle the gentle breeze.
Avocados, soft and bright,
Swirl around in pure delight.

Coconuts with hearty cheers,
Summon laughter through the years.
Friendly nuts all gather round,
In this space where joy is found.

Berries burst like giggling sprites,
Painting days with sweet delights.
Nature's fun, oh what a sight,
As colors blend from day to night.

Essence of Liveliness and Heartfelt Echoes

In the garden where vivacity thrives,
Fruits are humming, feeling alive.
Kiwis sharing witty lore,
While watermelons giggle and roar.

Peaches puff with rosy cheeks,
Deciding who the funniest speaks.
Strawberries burst with laughter bright,
Filling hearts with sheer delight.

Blackberries tumble with silly grace,
Racing in a fruity race.
Raspberries wink with mischief on hand,
As they plot a tale so grand.

Sass of citrus fills the air,
Jokes and jests are everywhere.
Each fruit moment, precious and rare,
Turns a garden into a fair.

The Bounty of Time Unveiled

In this bounty of playful days,
Fruits spin stories in funny ways.
Orchards laugh in sunny throngs,
Crooning sweet, silly songs.

Limes leap with a zingy cheer,
Telling tales for all to hear.
Peppers chuckle in vibrant hues,
Joining in with laughter's clues.

Plums play pranks beneath the trees,
Whispering softly to the bees.
Crisp apples twirl in joyous flight,
Bringing giggles and pure delight.

Every fruit bears joy to sow,
Through laughter, friendships overflow.
With nature's fun, our spirits soar,
As sweet days pass forevermore.

Pondering Under Leafy Canopies

I sat beneath a leafy tree,
Counting squirrels, one, two, three.
A bird flew by, dropped a pear,
Landed right in my messy hair!

The sunlight danced, a cheeky tease,
While ants marched by like tiny bees.
I pondered life with fruit in hand,
Debating snacks—what's really grand?

A lowly worm gave me a wink,
Should I eat or just rethink?
With every bite, my worries burst,
This fruity feast feels like a thirst!

So here I sit, with giggles spread,
Surrounded by fruit, no fear or dread.
Under the canopies, I grin wide,
In a silly mood, I shall abide!

Symphony of Ripened Dreams

Where fruits hang low, a tune begins,
A symphony of squishy skins.
With every pluck, a note is played,
A chorus formed with joyful grade!

A banana slips, oh what a show!
It slides away, oh no, oh no!
An orange rolls like a runaway,
Joining the fun in its own way.

The apples laugh, they jiggle around,
Creating beats upon the ground.
With every rhythm, laughter grows,
In this fruit concert, anything goes!

So I join in, playing air guitar,
With jammy fingers, I'm a star!
In this orchard stage, I sway and twirl,
A fruity dream, a silly whirl!

Seasons of Abundant Joy

The spring brings berries, plump and bright,
While summer melons steal the light.
In autumn, pumpkins roll and laugh,
And winter's citrus fruits are daft!

Each season laughs with fruity cheer,
In different shapes, both far and near.
A grape falls down, it starts to roll,
Pretending like it's in control!

The cherries gossip, juicy tales,
While peaches dance on windy trails.
With every season, oh what fun,
My fruity friends, they're never done!

A joyful picnic on a hill,
With laughter shared, a perfect thrill.
In nature's cycle, we partake,
Celebrating joy with every bake!

Palette of Sweet Endeavors

In a kitchen bright, where flavors blend,
I mix my fruit with laughter, friend.
Blueberries join the party line,
While honey drips like sunny wine.

A splash of lime, a sprinkle of zest,
Creating sweets that are the best.
A fruity cake, oh what a sight,
It giggles back in pure delight!

The oven hums a merry tune,
As my treats bake beneath the moon.
With every bite, my worries flee,
In this sweet world, it's just for me!

So grab a fork, don't be shy,
In this palette of joy, let's fly.
With fruity giggles and a pie,
We'll savor life, oh me, oh my!

Harvest of Moments

In a field of laughter, I trip on a pear,
Corn on the cob says, "Hey, don't you dare!"
The veggies are grinning, they know all the jokes,
While the fruits steal the show, like some sneaky folks.

Mangoes are lounging, taking a snooze,
Peach throws a party, but nobody's bruised.
Limes roll in laughter, they're zesty and bright,
While the apples debate who's the shiniest sight.

Grapes whisper secrets, oh what a thrill,
Bananas slip in, oh, give 'em a chill!
Cherry's on stage, with a crown on his head,
While Plum's in the corner, wishing he'd fled.

So raise up your glasses, let's toast to the fun,
To goofy old produce, our work here is done!
With humor and sweetness, let's dance through our days,
In this harvest of moments, we prank and we play!

Orchard of Time

In an orchard of giggles, where apples appear,
One fell from the branch, causing much cheer.
The cherries are bouncing, a playful brigade,
While the leaves join the dance in the sunlight cascade.

The oranges are juggling, so round and so bright,
While berries are plotting a cake for tonight.
Pears are winking as they sit on the green,
In this wacky old place, nothing's ever routine.

The crows crack a joke from the top of a tree,
While the squirrels provide all the acorn tea.
Even the sunlight can't help but to grin,
As shadows get tangled in the wild orchard spin.

So come take a stroll where the smiles are legit,
And join in the laughter, let's have a good sit.
With blossoms and giggles, and fruit in the breeze,
In this orchard of time, let's do as we please!

Bounty of Sunlit Hours

Underneath the sunshine, the fruits take a break,
Strawberries gossip, tossing in some cake.
The melons are lounging, too lazy to roll,
While the pumpkins are napping, enjoying their stroll.

The peaches are sculpting a statue of pie,
And lemons are painting a bright yellow sky.
Every hour blossoms with laughter and cheer,
As the fruits tell their tales, we all come to hear.

The apricots dance in a whirl of delight,
While the kiwi's freestyling, it's quite a sight!
The watermelon winks, with seeds on the side,
In the bounty of hours, we let joy be our guide.

We'll gather our giggles like nectar so sweet,
And feast on the laughter, it's such a good treat.
With sunshiny moments and days filled with cheer,
Let's savor this bounty, till the end of the year!

Whispers of the Seasonal Chill

As the air turns crisp, the veggies get bold,
Pumpkins don scarves, all orange and gold.
The carrots wear shades, feeling oh so fly,
While the cabbages chuckle, we won't tell them why.

The apples are planning a chill-out parade,
With cinnamon sips that are freshly homemade.
The pears toss around their hats and their coats,
In this funny old garden, we're all just good folks.

Now turnips, they're plotting, to dance on the street,
While radishes giggle, keeping cool on their feet.
The beets bring the rhythm, oh what a spree,
In whispers of chill, we'll laugh joyously.

So come bring your joy, as the frost starts to bite,
Let's savor our moments, oh what pure delight!
With humor and warmth, through the cold we will sail,
In the whispers of seasons, let's joyously prevail!

The Sweet Taste of Time's Gifts

In sunny grooves, we hop and skip,
With juicy thoughts, we take a trip.
A slice of laughter, a scoop of cheer,
Sprinkled with joy, we hold so dear.

Bananas dance in silly ways,
While pickles grin through crunchy haze.
Apple pies do pirouettes,
Tasting dreams one won't forget.

Mirthful laughter fills the air,
As peaches toss their fuzzy hair.
Time rolls on with fruity flair,
Creating treats beyond compare.

So raise a toast to silly days,
Where pineapple hats meet jelly rays.
In every bite, a wink of fate,
Our sweet delight, we celebrate!

Tales Shared in the Dappled Light

Under the tree, we spill our tales,
With juicy whispers on the trails.
A coconut cracks with a laugh so loud,
While cherries cheer, all brightly bowed.

We talk of pears in the summer sun,
And giggles shared in playful fun.
Melons roll with a hearty cheer,
Telling secrets for all to hear.

Bouncing berries join the spree,
While oranges sing, 'come dance with me!'
Collecting moments, sweet and bright,
Tales unfold in dappled light.

So gather 'round, let stories flow,
From fruity minds, let laughter grow.
In nature's lap, where joy ignites,
We weave the fabric of delight!

A Canopy of Joyful Reflections

Beneath the leaves, we find a space,
Where strawberries share their rosy grace.
With every giggle, breezes play,
A canopy where we laugh away.

Bright lemons burst in zesty song,
As silly thoughts bounce all day long.
A twist of lime, a wink from thyme,
Composing tunes, we dance in rhyme.

Grapes collide in a bouncing spree,
While funny tales cling to the tree.
Cherries toss their shiny heads,
Crafting humor, like comfy beds.

In this jungle of sheer delight,
The fruits and friends bring pure insight.
With every chuckle, with every glance,
Reflections bloom like a joyful dance!

Rich Seasons of Existence

In autumn's glow, the laughter swells,
With pumpkins sharing their giggled yells.
Carrots tap dance, all about,
While grapefruits giggle, 'what's this about?'

Spring blooms forth with zany flair,
As berries jiggle in the air.
Durian dreams with a funny face,
Blend with bananas in fruity grace.

Zucchini whispers with a cheeky grin,
While apples' laughter starts to spin.
The seasons shift, yet joy remains,
Wrapped in sweetness, like candy canes.

So here's to days that gleefully sway,
With magic fruits that laugh and play.
In every season, with joy we sow,
Rich moments bloom, as our hearts aglow!

Echoes Unfurled in Nature's Closet

In the garden, worms wear suits,
They march with pride among the roots.
A squirrel jogs with acorn weights,
While busy bees debate on dates.

The sun, a lazy, golden slouch,
Is snoozing on a cloud-shaped couch.
The rain plays tricks with puddle games,
And giggling frogs forget their names.

A crow in shades, with style so bold,
Caws tales of treasures yet untold.
While rabbits hop with floppy ears,
And dance away their silly fears.

Each day unfolds with quirks and charms,
Nature's antics bear no alarms.
From hesitant buds to fruits that sway,
Life's comedy brings smiles each day.

Fables of Forgotten Time

Once a peach wore a silly hat,
Claiming it could help with chat.
An apple joked of being round,
While teasing pears, who fell and frowned.

The grape danced solo on the vine,
While berries bickered, topsy-turvy line.
Old figs, wise, with wrinkled smiles,
Spun stories full of wily styles.

A carrot, dressed in bright parade,
Claimed it was the top of the spade.
While lettuce longed to be the queen,
But kale just laughed, a shady scene.

In every bite, a tale resides,
Of laughter shared on fun-filled rides.
With every crunch, a giggle springs,
As nature hums, and merriment sings.

A Dance of Abundant Days

The sun peeped in with a cheesy grin,
As daisies twirled in their bright spin.
A shallot tried to start a band,
But onions cried, "We can't stand!"

Tomatoes whispered, "Let's take flight!"
While herbs debated, day or night.
The carrots cartwheeled, sweet and bold,
In this dance, a sight to behold.

Berries bounced with flair and zest,
Their fruity moves were surely best.
With every twirl, a splash of cheer,
Nature's party thrived each year!

From morning light to twilight's hue,
These capers bloom with laughter too.
Days are ripe with jests, all we say,
Join nature's dance and play each day.

Gathering Nourishment from Life's Garden

In the patch, a lettuce plays tag,
While peppers boast of their green swag.
Radishes giggle, hiding fast,
Yet trumpets blare—it's veggie cast!

The squash gets tangled in the vine,
Says, "I'm fashion; I'm divine!"
Cauliflowers wore crowns of fluff,
But cabbage grinned, "I'm tough enough!"

Basil and thyme formed a rock band,
With rhythms spun across the land.
While carrots sported shades of bright,
And turned the day into pure delight.

Each harvest brings a quirky tale,
Of laughter sung on every trail.
For every bite and giggle shared,
Life's garden blooms, fully prepared.

Rituals of Sunshine and Sweetness

Morning giggles, toasted bread,
Smiles spreading like jam on spread.
Pancakes flip, syrup's a dance,
In this feast, we take a chance.

Lemonade sips in the blazing heat,
Laughter bubbles, oh so sweet.
Honey bees join in the fun,
Chasing shadows under the sun.

Picnic plans with ants on the prowl,
Sandwiches vanish, yet we howl.
Watermelon slurps, juice on our chin,
Every bite a cheeky grin.

In the twilight, dance till we drop,
Plums in hand, we'll never stop.
Life's ripe fruit, a comedy show,
Sweetness scattered, let laughter flow.

Shades of Joy in Each Waking Hour

Morning banter with coffee in sight,
Cereal spills, oh what a sight!
Chasing socks that refuse to pair,
Mismatched feet, we just don't care.

Lunchbox treasures, surprises inside,
Carrots winking, we giggle wide.
Tuna fish chats with pickles that dance,
Every bite brings a laugh and a chance.

Sunset picnics, under stars that pop,
Jellybeans gifted, they never stop.
Running races on soft, green grass,
Who knew joy could come with a splash?

Upside-down smiles from ripe fruit we find,
Jokes exchanged with each double-dined.
Every hour's a riot, odd and bright,
Shades of joy in each silly bite.

Edibles Gathered from Nature's Hands

Nature's bounty fills the plate,
Funny faces as we taste fate.
Toothy grins with peachy bliss,
Each fruit seems to say, "Don't miss!"

Cherry giggles and grapes that wink,
Smoothies blend with a fizzy drink.
Lettuce leaf tickles, what a sight!
Vegetables join us in delight.

Berries bounce like little balls,
Cucumber laughter as nature calls.
Harvesting joy from sun and soil,
In funny ways, our hearts we spoil.

Under moonlight, veggies joke loud,
Broccolis dressed in silly shrouds.
Every meal a humorous blend,
Nature's gifts, our laughter's friend.

The Beauty of Harvesting Laughter

Fields of giggles in the sun,
Gathering joy, it's never done.
Pumpkins grinning, claiming the throne,
In this harvest, we feel at home.

Corn mazes twist like laughter's song,
Running through, you can't go wrong.
Snap peas pop like jokes in the air,
Mirthful moments, with friends to share.

Berry patches, sweeter than dreams,
Silly faces in our berry schemes.
Foot races through the orchard trees,
Every stumble brings on the tease.

As we gather, smiles take flight,
Even in darkness, we're filled with light.
Harvesting laughter, a beautiful chase,
In life's garden, humor finds its place.

The Rich Aroma of Golden Memories

Once I found a pear so sweet,
It danced beneath my happy feet.
A grape just winked, it had a tale,
Of how it dreamed of being ale.

The apples giggled, plump and round,
They asked me where my joy was found.
I said, in laughter, juice, and cheer,
With fruity friends, life's sweet and clear.

Bananas slipped with grand delight,
A comic scene, oh what a sight!
We made a punch, a splendid mix,
With seeds of humor, all the tricks.

This fruity crew, they never stop,
In every laugh and jumping hop.
In every slice, the memories bloom,
In juicy corners, there's always room.

Tasting Wisdom from Nature's Feast

I bit a peach, it blew my mind,
With every bite, joy I did find.
It whispered secrets, oh so sweet,
Of summer days and sunny heat.

The berries mocked, in vibrant hues,
They claimed to know the best life views.
"Just taste and grin, don't ask too much,"
For wisdom comes as nature's touch.

I met a fig, so sly and smart,
Gave me a lesson on living art.
"Be rich in flavor, not in fear,
For time is fleeting, my dear, my dear."

With every fruit, a tale unfurled,
Of laughter, joy—a funny world.
Each bite a giggle, full of glee,
Nature's feast—come dine with me!

Sun-Kissed Moments in the Shade

Oh, a coconut fell right on my head,
Woke me from a dream where I fed.
To oranges dressed in sunshine bright,
Who brought the zest to wrongs and right.

Lemons laughed, with a sass so bold,
"Life's sour, darling, don't be controlled!"
I took a sip of lemonade cheer,
And danced away all worry and fear.

Pineapples pranced, with tops held high,
"Let's make a party, come on, don't be shy!"
With every drop, we twirled and spun,
In shaded joy, where fruit always won.

These sunny moments, they slip away,
But memories linger, come what may.
With fruits of laughter, let's fill our days,
In the shade of fun, let's forever play!

The Rainbow of Experience

In a bowl of color, stories gleam,
Where cherries blush and peaches beam.
Every hue a different laugh,
A wild adventure down the path.

The blueberries told of midnight skies,
While strawberries shared with twinkling eyes.
"Just taste the wild, the weird, the fun,
In every munch, there's a story spun!"

Kiwis giggled, all green and bright,
"Embrace the odd, it feels just right!"
Each crunchy bite, a chuckle, a roar,
Of lessons learned and joys galore.

With every shade, a memory lies,
In laughter's hues, we synthesize.
So join this feast, where smiles cascade,
In the rainbow of moments, we all parade.

Enchanted Days in Bloom

In a garden full of daisies bright,
A squirrel danced with all his might.
He wore a hat made of ripe figs,
And pranced around like silly prigs.

The bees were buzzing quite a tune,
While frogs croaked loudly under the moon.
A ladybug rode a butterfly high,
Both laughing as they painted the sky.

Each petal seemed to tell a joke,
As flowers giggled under the oak.
The breeze was tickling every face,
It whispered secrets with such grace.

And every day, we laugh and play,
In this land of dreams, we live and stay.
With joy and cheer, our hearts do bloom,
Creating fun in every room.

Savoring the Apple of Today

A bite of red so crisp and sweet,
Made me jump up and tap my feet.
The juiciest fruit that ever existed,
With laughter and joy, I softly insisted.

Around the tree, a party unfurled,
With chatter and giggles from all the world.
The worms had hats, and apples wore shoes,
It was a feast, filled with colorful hues.

But then came a pie, wild and round,
It rolled away with a giggling sound.
Chasing it down, we all fell in line,
Laughter erupted, it was simply divine!

So let's munch on this feast of delight,
With every bite, our hearts feel light.
We'll savor today with giggles and cheer,
And hope tomorrow will be just as dear.

Chasing the Sun's Warm Embrace

Running barefoot in the meadows so wide,
We chased the sun, with arms open wide.
A race with sunshine, who'd take the lead?
Giggling children, oh, what a creed!

The flowers waved as we dashed on by,
The clouds above just drifting, oh my!
With icy treats made of rainbow swirl,
Kites flew high as our laughter twirled.

Worms wearing ties joined in the fun,
They wriggled and wobbled, almost on the run.
Faces smeared with chocolate delight,
Sun-kissed hair shimmered in the bright light.

We'll welcome each day with playful cheer,
As we chase the sun, our hearts sincere.
In this glorious game of chase and race,
We find the joy in every embrace.

Nature's Serenade of Bliss

In the forest, where squirrels sing,
A chorus of laughter the tree tops bring.
Birds in tuxedos, chirping with glee,
Nature's own concert, just for you and me.

A raccoon with bells performs a jig,
While rabbits hop, oh, look at that pig!
Each leaf rustles with jokes from the trees,
As nature tickles the tummy with ease.

The sun winks down, like a cheeky lad,
Creating shadows that dance with the mad.
The grass beneath laughs as we roll,
In the theater of life, we all play a role.

So let's join this song, so vibrant and true,
With each playful note, our spirits renew.
In this perfect blend of joy and cheer,
Nature's serenade is crystal clear.